Contents

I0409952

Scenario   1

Introduction   3

The Terrorist Threat to the Homeland   4

The Proliferation and Availability of Sea Mines   7

U.S. Mine Countermeasures Posture   8

Counterargument   12

Conclusion   15

Recommendations   16

Bibliography   19

Notes   21

I0409952

We will not permit conditions under which our maritime forces would be impeded from freedom of maneuver and freedom of access, nor will we permit an adversary to disrupt the global supply chain by attempting to block vital sea-lines of communication and commerce.[1]

A Cooperative Strategy for 21st Century Sea Power

Sea mining is one of the least expensive, easiest to employ, and most highly effective methods for an adversary to deny sea control to a major sea power. It is therefore most alarming, in this era of increasing anti-U.S. terrorist activity, that the current U.S. Navy's mine countermeasures (MCM) posture falls critically short of achieving the necessary peacetime conditions to effectively counter mine threats along its Atlantic seaboard and Gulf coast. Consider the following scenario that reflects this assertion.

Scenario

On December 31st, 2013, as the sun rises over the Atlantic Ocean, cargo vessels awaiting inspection in the approaches to the Chesapeake Bay off Norfolk, VA, transmit frantic distress calls to port security and the United States Coast Guard station at Portsmouth, VA. The reports are chilling as they detail the sighting by deckhands and captains of over fifteen objects resembling WWII era contact mines in and around their anchorages. Later that afternoon an oil tanker importing crude oil to a Houston, Texas refinery strikes a mine in the Gulf of Mexico, just thirteen miles off the coast. The mine has not only sunk the ship but also triggered a secondary explosion that killed the entire crew and spilled millions of gallons of petroleum into the Gulf of Mexico. Uncertain as to whether or not more mines have been deployed in the area, spill containment vessels are unable to safely respond to isolate the spill and initiate clean-up efforts. Heavy onshore winds threaten to push the oil landward to the Texas beaches and estuaries in a matter of days.

Later the same evening, pilot vessels out of Earl, New Jersey and New York discover three abandoned fishing trawlers all containing numerous empty crates built to house manta-type bottom mines. All shipping is halted and U.S. Navy vessels conducting ammunition upload at Earl are effectively blockaded in port.

The following day an Al Qaeda sleeper cell claims responsibility for the mining via an internet manifesto, declaring that the attack was an act of vengeance for the "murder" of Osama bin Laden. An international crisis has unfolded, a terrorist splinter cell has seized the initiative, and sea control in the home waters of the world's most powerful navy is now lost.

The U.S. Navy must respond or national and world markets will falter, potentially triggering worldwide economic crisis. With the nearest U.S. MCM ship stationed in San Diego the estimated transit to on-station timeline presented to the Secretary of Defense is an alarming thirty days.[2] Furthermore, metrological conditions for the next four days include moderate rain, poor visibility and near freezing temperatures that will keep Norfolk, VA based Airborne Mine Countermeasures (AMCM) helicopters grounded for the next four days. In short, the United States of America is unable to effectively respond to the attack and the world's greatest navy has lost control the sea lines of communication (SLOC) with in its territorial seas.

While the preceding scenario is fictitious and fabricated specifically for this paper, it is nonetheless very much realistic and plausible. Accordingly, from this narrative it is fair to assert that the current U.S. MCM force posture constitutes a concerning inability to respond in a timely manner to a sea mining event in our nation's home waters.

Introduction

In the 2010 National Security Strategy (NSS), President Obama's first listed enduring interest of the United States is "the security of the United States and its citizens."[3] This direction is highlighted in the Joint Publication for Homeland Defense (HD), JP 3-27, which notes that "defense of the homeland is the Department of Defense's (DOD) highest priority."[4] Furthermore, JP 3-27 identifies two of the key HD objectives as (1) "ensure defense of the homeland and deny an adversary's access to the nation's sovereign airspace, territory and territorial seas," and (2) "recover from any attack or incident."[5] Nevertheless, perennial budgetary neglect and a mismanagement of the basic operational art concept of balancing the factors Space, Time, and Force have combined to expose U.S. Navy MCM capacity as a critical vulnerability to U.S. maritime national security. The challenge of balancing these factors, as they relate to MCM capabilities, will become even more daunting in the immediate future due to nationally mandated budget sequestration. Sequestration will not only restrict legacy MCM asset maintenance and operational tempo, but also further impede already behind schedule development of future MCM assets. However, by focusing on current direction outlined in national security and defense directives, leveraging existing multinational defense relationships, and continuing Theater Security Cooperation (TSC) initiatives, there is potential for

Geographic Combatant Commanders (GCC) to achieve increased efficiency in global

MCM response while concurrently fortifying homeland defense MCM capacity.

This paper will address the threat of terrorist mine warfare in U.S. waters and the

Navy's MCM shortfall in fulfilling its homeland defense role. To gain a better frame of

reference for the problem, an overview of the terrorist mine threat will be discussed first.

Next the current U.S. MCM force composition and posture will be assessed as it relates

to standing directives and emerging threats. Finally, recommendations to strengthen the

MCM response capacity for homeland defense as well as U.S. Central Command

(CENTCOM) and U.S. Pacific Command (PACOM) capacity to protect U.S. interests

abroad.

The Threat to the Homeland

Question: How many mines does it take to create a minefield?
Answer: None, it just takes the threat of a mine.
Anonymous

Though the above epigraph may appear to some to be a riddle of little significance

when it comes to the issue of homeland defense, maritime freedom of maneuver and

mine countermeasures it is a reality that must be planned for. Historically, prudence has

dictated that the risk of dismissing unverified reports of sea mining activity outweighs the

reward of blind continuation of sea-lane transit assuming or hoping the mining threat was

an empty one. However, this prudence and caution comes at a cost as discovered during

the January 1980 "patriotic scuba diver" event described below that targeted California's

Sacramento River.

An unknown person identifying himself as "the patriotic scuba diver" claimed by telephone to have placed a mine in the waterway; all shipping movement was ceased almost immediately. Once on the scene, the Navy minesweeper USS *Gallant* required four days of intensive mine hunting to determine the channel was safe. No mines were discovered, but the cost in merchant vessel lay days caused by the hoax was estimated in the hundreds of thousands of dollars.[6]

As shown here, a mere telephonic threat of sea mining in a narrow area can delay commerce for nearly a week and induce a significant economic impact. Nevertheless, the cost of a mine strike continues to outweigh the benefit of attempting uninterrupted trade in waters of questionable security. For this reason mines pose a credible, inexpensive and easily deployed threat to U.S. security and terrorists comprehend this.

The most significant precedent for a terrorist like deployment of sea mines on a grand scale can be found in the 1984 "Mines of August" incident. During this incident some twenty-three vessels reported undersea explosions across Red Sea and Gulf of Suez waters in the wake of an unknown actor's mining operations. Ultimately mine countermeasures vessels and aircraft from Egypt, France, Great Britain, Italy, the Netherlands, the Soviet Union, and the United States combined efforts and cleared the waterways; though they only found and exploited one mine. Sometime later it was proven that the mines had been haphazardly deployed from a ferry ship over a period of two weeks by Libyan navy personnel.[7]

The "Mines of August" incident illustrates the ease at which untrained personnel, haphazardly shoving mines over the side of a civil vessel, can bring maritime freedom of maneuver to its knees. While that event occurred in foreign waters it could just as easily have occurred in U.S. territorial seas as described in the opening scenario of this paper. Speaking to the current realism of this threat, former Chairman of the Committee on

Foreign Relations, then Senator John Kerry, noted in his January 2010 report to the U.S. Senate that Al Qaeda has evolved to become a terrorist threat not only abroad but also within the contiguous United States.[8] He goes on to emphasize that Al Qaeda's "recruitment tactics have changed, such that radicalized American citizens, converted to Islam, are now being recruited to carry out attacks within our borders." Adding further credence to this claim, the same document quotes John Brennan, then Assistant to the President for Homeland Security and Counterterrorism, who in a 2009 speech stated "Al Qaeda has proven to be adaptive and highly resilient and remains the most serious terrorist threat we face as a nation."[9]

Driving this point home is the April 15th, 2013, terrorist bombing at the Boston Marathon that was carried out by just two Islamic extremists using improvised explosive devices fashioned out of pressure cookers. This low-tech asymmetric attack was executed without detection as the terrorists easily blended into the crowd much the same way mine laden fishing trawlers could blend into the normal maritime traffic in major port approaches critical to U.S. economic stability. The attack in Boston reaffirms the notion that the United States will, for the foreseeable future, be engaged in constant battle with a broad range of terrorist organizations. Without a doubt, these actors will continue to pursue increasingly diverse asymmetric methods, making the possibility of improvised sea mines constructed using oil drums or refrigerators a very real threat to the homeland.

Reflecting on the Boston attack, New York City Police Commissioner Ray Kelly, who created the country's first municipal counterterrorism bureau in the wake of 9/11, asserted that "When something like Boston happens, it's a shock to the public psyche, but not to us. We thought something like this would happen sooner—we've seen these types of disaffected radicalized young men target us."[10] In fact his bureau has thwarted 16 terror plots since the attacks on the World Trade Center in September 2001.[11]

Specifically addressing the terrorist sea mine threat to U.S. waterways, recognized national security consultant Dr. Daniel Goure points out that "it is important that national decisionmakers [sic] appreciate the fact that sea mines in contested waters or in and around ports could constitute a 'show stopper'."[12] It is thus well established that terrorists have the access and means required to seed mines in the domestic waterways of the United States but what about the availability of the mines themselves? How easily are they acquired?

The Proliferation and Availability of Sea Mines

Sea mines remain the Achilles Heel of our Navy![13]
Gordon England
Former Secretary of the Navy

As professed by recognized naval theorist Doctor Milan Vego, the principal operational warfare objective for a major sea power such as the Unites States is to establish and maintain a particular degree of sea control in the Maritime Theater of Operations.[14] Consequently, one of the least expensive, easiest to employ, and most highly effective methods for an adversary to deny sea control to a major sea power is sea mining.

The types of sea mines available to 21st century terrorists are vast and the inventory plentiful. In fact, "more than a quarter-million sea mines of more than 300 types are in the inventories of more than fifty navies world wide. Additionally, more than thirty countries produce mines and more than twenty countries export mines. Even highly sophisticated weapons are available in the international arms trade."[15] Furthermore, mines available in the international arms trade or black markets can be simply purchased on a "cash-and-carry basis."[16]

As the sophistication and lethality of mines continue to evolve, more and more old technology mines will likely populate the market as countries such as China, Russia, North Korea, and Iran update their inventories. These countries' surplus inventories of outdated yet still operable mines are prime for marketing to terrorists seeking low-cost asymmetric weapons. Make no mistake, the fact that these mines are old and low-tech does not render them any less dangerous. In fact, the mines that the USS *Samuel Roberts* and the USS *Tripoli* stuck in 1988 and 1991 respectively, were primitive contact mines commonly purchased for less than $1500. Despite these mines' bargain basement price tag and pre-WWII era technology, they achieved their objective, taking both ships out of the fight and inflicting a combined $110 million in damages.[17] The mine that the *Tripoli* struck was part of Saddam Hussein's substantial inventory and one can reasonably assume that with the fall of his regime some of that inventory of has since made it into the hands of terrorists or black market weapons brokers.[18]

U.S. Mine Countermeasures Posture

The great danger is that if mine countermeasures continues to be neglected, large wartime appropriations for countermeasures will be almost useless because the fundamental development will still have to be done first.[19]

Admiral Forrest P. Sherman
Former Chief of Naval Operations

The current U.S. Navy dedicated mine countermeasures force consists of three basic components, commonly referred to as the MCM Triad. In broad terms the Triad is composed of *Avenger* class surface MCM ships (SMCM), MH-53E airborne MCM (AMCM) helicopters, and explosive ordinance disposal (EOD) teams that operate remote MCM vehicles and employ marine mammal MCM assets. Generally speaking the Triad is employed in a manner such that the SMCM vessels and AMCM helicopters conduct mine hunting and sweeping mission in water depths of 40 feet and greater while the EOD personnel conduct MCM in very shallow water depths of 40 feet or less. Additionally, EOD assets are often employed to prosecute mines that have been located by the SMCM and AMCM assets. Beyond this legacy capability, the Navy has in development unmanned underwater and surface vehicles as well as a limited MH-60S helicopter AMCM capability that is to be deployed aboard Littoral Combat Ships (LCS). However, various delays, setbacks, and failures have retarded projected fleet integration dates for these capabilities.[20] As a result these new technology assets are not projected to enter initial operational test and evaluation (IOT&E) until mid-2014 at the earliest.[21] Ultimately the full operational capability of the LCS squadrons with associated MCM mission packages will not likely be realized until 2020 or beyond.[22] What this equates to is that for the remainder of this decade, U.S. MCM operations in depths greater than 40 feet will have to rely on the lot of twenty-two legacy MH-53E AMCM helicopters and thirteen *Avenger* class SMCMs. These assets are currently deployed as such:

MH-53E AMCM helicopters*

Qty	Location
• 15	Norfolk, VA (distributed between HM-14, HM-15 and AWSTS)
• 4	Manama, Bahrain
• 3	Pohang, Republic of Korea

* Note that at any time approximately 1/3 of these assets are likely to be non-mission capable due to required planned maintenance cycles of varying levels.

Avenger **Class SMCM ships**[23][24]

	Qty	Location
•	6	Manama, Bahrain
•	4	Sasebo, Japan
•	3	San Diego, CA

As shown above, the east coast of the United States is devoid of a single surface MCM asset and supported by only a handful of AMCM assets located in Norfolk. Notably, AMCM assets are restricted to day only MCM operations in environments clear of icing conditions.[25] Additional restrictions to AMCM's employment are ceiling and visibility limitations of no lower than 500 feet above ground level and 2 nautical miles respectively.[26] These restrictions combine to make operating windows in winter months especially narrow considering shorter periods of daylight and an increased propensity for the occurrence of icing conditions.

SMCMs, on the other hand, have the ability operate day and night with fewer metrological restrictions. Though the SMCMs lack speed when conducting their mission, their ability to remain on station in the minefield for days on end is a favorable trade off. Despite SMCMs advantages, they have a critical flaw, that being reliability. Highlighting the SMCM track record of poor mission readiness, a 2010 assessment task force found that of the fourteen U.S. SMCMs inspected, only one was capable of getting underway and fully executing its MCM missions.[27] An additional vulnerability when considering SMCMs is their slow transit speed of approximately 10 knots. Thus, the timeline for movement of these assets from a base of operations or homeport to the area of operations is a critical vulnerability to be considered by planners at all levels. As described in this paper's scenario, movement of an SMCM from San Diego to Norfolk would realistically take thirty days or more, depending on metrological conditions.

Confronted with limited operational assets, setbacks in test and development of new systems, and increased threat levels in the CENTCOM and PACOM AORs, GCCs and senior Department of Defense (DOD) officials face the difficult task of allocating MCM resources across the globe to counter the most menacing threats. Accordingly, a 2012 request for forces (RFF) ballooned MCM asset presence in the CENTCOM AOR, poised to counter Iranian threats in the vicinity of the Strait of Hormuz. As a result, the United States' HD posture with respect to MCM has been severely degraded. While this no doubt is a calculated risk assumed by senior DOD leadership, it is nonetheless cautioned against in the 2010 NSS that specifically points out that "our enemies aim to overextend our Armed Forces."[28]

As such, the forward deployment of nearly our entire MCM surface fleet to the CENTCOM and PACOM AORs, in response to Iranian saber rattling in the Strait of Hormuz and the standing contingency posture in the western Pacific, has left the current U.S. MCM forces acutely deficient in their ability to provide a timely and effective response to crisis scenarios in U.S. territorial waters. Most concerning regarding the poor state of the MCM readiness and coverage along the U.S. coasts and waterways, is that the Navy is the sole domestic resource of this capability. Simply put, there is no other maritime mine warfare capability or agency to fall back on for this void in security.

For this reason, GCCs must appropriately consider the concept of economy of force when shaping the DOD's posture to conduct homeland defense operations. Economy of force allows the commander to judiciously focus the necessary forces on the primary objective. In turn, only the minimal essential assets are to be allocated for achieving secondary objectives. Hand-in-hand with economy of force are the critical operational functions of *movement* and *maneuver (M2)*. The commander's ability to effectively conduct M2 reflects the timeliness with which he can bring required forces into a theater of operations and then project forward this combat power to directly engage the threat.[29] This is the challenge presented by the U.S. Navy's relatively small and aged legacy SMCM force that is handicapped with glacial movement characteristics and historic full mission capable rates of well below 25 percent.

The NSS clearly communicates that the primary objective for the DOD is HD with the implied mission of ensuring the security of national economic maritime thoroughfares. Therefore, keeping the HD mission clearly at the forefront when developing and updating theater campaign plans is essential.

Counterargument

One may argue that the U.S. Navy's forward deployed posture is of greater strategic importance than keeping a credible MCM force in CONUS, standing by for a maritime terror event to respond to. Frequently, MCM conversations turn to the importance of patrolling the Arabian Gulf and the Strait of Hormuz that, according to the U.S. Energy Information Administration, serves as the sea-lane for approximately 20 percent of world seaborne petroleum trade.[30] To this end, conventional belief is that a mining event in the Strait of Hormuz would result in catastrophic effects on the global economy.

While the Strait or Hormuz and its surrounding waters certainly serve as major energy thoroughfare, the impact that mining would have on world petroleum markets is unclear. In fact, in the heat of the 1984 Red Sea/Gulf of Suez mine crisis, commercial and naval traffic continued to transit the sea-lanes unabated, despite reports of underwater

explosions. The ultimate effect was that, while the incident did cause a fluctuation in

insurance rates, the world petroleum prices were virtually unaffected.[31]

Further analyzing the effects of this event, Commander Rodney Mills wrote the

following in a 2008 Naval War College study on mine warfare.

> Conventional wisdom might suggest that the initiation of hostilities in the Strait
> of Hormuz or Persian Gulf would stop or significantly deter the flow of maritime
> traffic through the strait but the 'Tanker Wars' between Iran and Iraq in 1980s
> show a different behavior by the shipping industry. During the eight years of the
> conflict, 544 attacks were carried out against all shipping in the gulf resulting in
> more than 400 civilians killed and another 400 injured. However, after an initial
> 25 percent drop, the shipping industry adjusted to the risk and the flow of
> commerce resumed. Despite the threat, oil and other maritime commerce
> continued to flow even as the conflict intensified through 1987, when a total of
> 179 attacks were carried out, or roughly an attack every other day.[32]

Thus, predictions that even temporary disruptions of tanker traffic could "cause

global oil prices to soar and spark widespread economic turmoil" appear to be over

trumpeted.[33]

Furthermore, as figure 1 shows, oil that transits the Strait of Hormuz accounts for

only 9 percent of the United States' oil consumption. In contrast, the Strait of Hormuz is

a choke point for the passage of 92 percent of South Korea's oil, 82 percent of

Singapore's, 71 percent of India's, and 64 percent of Japan's. Considering these figures,

and the fact that each of these countries possess a credible MCM force, it seems

inappropriate that the U.S. has invested its MCM assets so heavily in the Arabian Gulf

region. The consequence of the United States' forward deployed MCM posture is

incurrence of considerable risk to the defense of domestic ports along the U.S. eastern

seaboard and in the Gulf of Mexico. In light of this risk, a complete withdrawal of MCM

capabilities in the Arabian Gulf region is by no means a prudent course of action.

However, the U.S. may do well to pursue increased load sharing in the CENTCOM AOR

with the above-mentioned naval forces as well as European coalition partner navies.

Noteworthy to this discussion, the North Atlantic Treaty Organization maintains Standing

Mine Countermeasures Groups (SNMCMG) with SMCM assets that could be well

complimented with the AMCM capabilities the U.S. maintains in Bahrain.

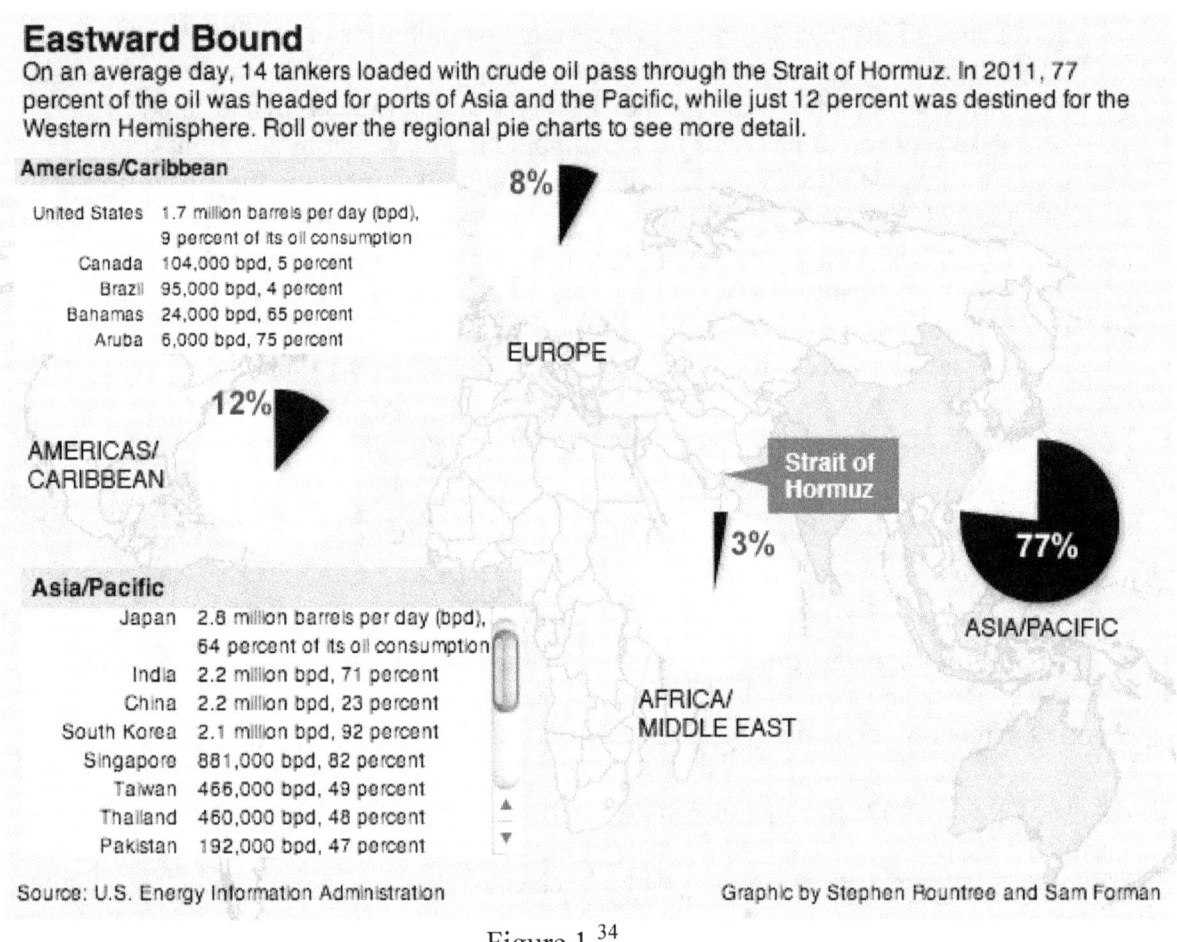

Figure 1.[34]

While the exact economic impact of a mining event in the Strait of Hormuz is

disputed, the economic impact of a port shutdown in the United States would no doubt be

catastrophic. National security expert Scott Truver points out that with "'America's

globalized, just-in-time, and just-enough economy' just a few mines would likely result

in a $1.95 billion (2002 dollars) impact per day."[35] Not factored in this economic impact analysis is the environmental devastation that would result from the sinking of super

tanker in the territorial waters of the United States. As demonstrated by the BP

DEEPWATER HORIZON and EXXON VALDEZ incidents, the uncontrolled release of

petroleum product into the fragile marine ecosystems will devastate not only marine life,

but also the regional economies that are anchored in the coastal beaches' tourism and

seafood industry.

Conclusion

Leadership and planners have always faced the dilemma of parsing limited

resources amongst multiple competing interests. Well-formed decisions on when, where,

and how to apply those limited resources are based on adherence to validated national

strategic directive, maximizing force effectiveness and flexibility by managing *Space,*

Time, and *Force*, and ultimately, accepting an appropriate level of risk only where the

benefit outweighs the cost. This dilemma is becoming more acute for the national

defense leadership as U.S. DOD budgets are reduced, personnel are drawn down, and

fleet implementation of new MCM technology continues to lag behind originally

anticipated timelines and capabilities.[36]/[37]

The existing direction for MCM as it relates to HD, outlined in multiple doctrinal

documents to include the NSS and the Joint Publication for Homeland Defense is,

without question, prudent. However, despite the validity of this published direction, U.S.

DOD leadership has allowed tensions abroad in the CENTCOM and PACOM AORs to

compromise NORTHCOM's HD mission. As a result, the economic, environmental, and physical security of the U.S. Atlantic and Gulf Coasts has been placed in increased jeopardy.

A credible MCM capability is much like a life insurance policy; it is a necessary investment in protection that one hopes one will never have to use. Nonetheless, the policy that is purchased must be of sufficient composition and appropriately scaled to ensure the policyholder's beneficiaries will be provided a requisite amount of coverage when an incident does occur and a claim must be filed. As such, the current U.S. MCM "insurance policy" is not sufficiently scaled to provide the necessary balance of *Space, Time,* and *Force* requisite to satisfy national security priorities as detailed in the NSS. In effect the U.S. HD MCM posture is a cut-rate policy with a high deductible, incapable of efficiently satisfying the nation's needs in a crisis scenario.

Recognizing this need, U.S. GCCs must develop and collectively promote a more cooperative maritime strategy that sufficiently prioritizes timely response in defending homeland waters above all else. By securing the defense of the homeland first, forward deploying forces to address specific emergent threats to national security second, and positioning to support a multinational force to defend international sea lines of communication last, U.S. Commanders will better leverage legacy MCM capabilities to achieve national and international objectives.

Recommendations

1) To address the terrorist sea mine threat on the U.S. Atlantic and Gulf coasts, a minimum of two SMCM vessels should be stationed in Norfolk, VA and another two SMCM vessels should be stationed in the Gulf Coast region.

2) Better leverage our allies' and friends' capabilities at the operational and tactical level to multiply capacity and facilitate flexibility in the means used to achieve national and international desired end states. Specifically in the realm of MCM, CENTCOM and PACOM might consider pursuing a shift in the preponderance of responsibility for SMCM capabilities to NATO, the United Kingdom, India, Singapore, Thailand, Australia, South Korea, and Japan. As evident in figure 1, many of these countries have especially vested interest in the free flow of oil out of the Arabian Gulf. Accomplishing this would allow a portion of forward deployed SMCMs to be redeployed to Atlantic and Gulf Coast ports to support NORTHCOM's HD mission. With this goal in mind, TSC, military-to-military engagement, and multinational Exercises will continue to serve as strategic enablers to sustaining a flexible multi-national global MCM crisis response capability. This sentiment is echoed in the DOD's *Priorities for 21st Century Defense* that affirms the need, in the current era of federal fiscal constraint, to "promote enhanced capacity and interoperability for coalition operations."[38] In doing so, allied nation capabilities can readily be "pooled and shared to create a "Smart Defense" in the face of 21st century challenges."[39]

In fact this initiative is already well developed with respect to mine warfare in the earlier discussed North Atlantic Treaty Organization's Standing Mine Countermeasures Groups. Operating in two groups, SNMCMG1 and SNMCMG2 provide multinational MCM forces responsible for the waters in and around the Northern Atlantic and the Mediterranean. This multinational force operates under one common doctrine. As such, twelve nations contribute MCM assets under a unified command and control structure to "perform different tasks ranging from participating in exercises to actually intervening in operational missions," providing a "continuous maritime capability for operations and other activities in peacetime and in periods of crisis and conflict."[40]

3) Continue to emphasize Theater Security Cooperation efforts. TSC plays a critical role in the path to economic and security stability across the global commons. Current U.S. doctrine recognizes and promotes this idea as it stresses continuous development and refinement of multinational operations planning.[41] This planning must encompass not only courses of action for combat operations, but also non-combat operations and contingency response to terrorist activities. The primacy of TSC is reflected in President Obama's NSS which notes that while the United States of America will "continue to underwrite global security" it is imperative to reaffirm the notion that "no one nation can meet global challenges alone."[42]

4) Verify that the Guidance for the Employment of the Force (GEF) sufficiently reflects the terrorist threat as it relates to HD and Homeland Security. As the GEF feeds the Joint Strategic Capabilities Plan, leadership must additionally verify that GCC tasking contained there in is not in conflict with resources and forces apportioned to another GCC. As the size of our armed force is reduced this concern will likely place strain on the maintenance of current Operational and Concept Plans as well as the future development of the same. Difficult choices will have to be made in prioritizing resource apportionment in the Global Force Management Implementation Guidance. All the

while, the "Adaptive Planning" review processes must reflect changes to the NSS, desired end states, and dynamic threats to national security interests.

Parting Remarks

The Chief of Naval Operations (CNO) approved Mine Warfare lesson learned from Operation DESERT STORM specifies "the need for a robust, deployable U.S. Navy MCM capability."[43] In response, then CNO Admiral Kelso pledged an in-depth strategy and readiness review "to ensure our ability to conduct independent mine countermeasures operations when required."[44] Yet, contrary to ADM Kelso's findings, the Navy decommissioned all twelve *Osprey* class mine hunting ships between 2006 and 2007[45], which, when combined with mishap attrition of *Avenger* class SMCM and MH-53E AMCM assets, has left current MCM readiness significantly *degraded* when compared to the DESERT STORM era level. Thus, while the Navy was undoubtedly *taught* a MCM lesson in DESERT STORM, it does not appear that this lesson has ever truly been *learned*. As a result, the current MCM posture presents a critical vulnerability to U.S. maritime security and the HD mission.

Notes

1 Chief of Naval Operations, *A Cooperative Strategy for 21st Century Seapower* (Washington, DC: United States Department of the Navy, 2007), 10.

2 National Geospatial Intelligence Agency, *Distances Between Ports,* (Bethesda, MD: National Geospatial Intelligence Agency, 2001), 71, 95.

3 The White House, *National Security Strategy,* (Washington, D.C.: GPO, 2010), 7.

4 Chairman, Joint Chiefs of Staff. *Homeland Defense.* Joint Publication (JP), (Washington, DC: Department of Defense, CJCS, July 12, 2007), vii.

5 Ibid, viii.

6 Mark Tempest, "Port Security: Sea Mines, UWIEDS and Other Threats," *EagleSpeak.* May 1, 2008, http://observer.guardian.co.uk/waronterrorism/story /0,1373,624278,00.html, 4.

7 Scott C. Truver, "Mines and Underwater IEDs in U.S. Ports and Waterways: Context, Threats, Challenges, and Solutions," *Naval War College Review* Vol. 61 no.1 (Winter 2008), 111.

8 Committee on Foreign Relations, United States Senate, *Al Qaeda in Yemen and Somalia a Ticking Time Bomb: A Report to the Committee on Foreign Relations, United States Senate, One Hundred Eleventh Congress, Second Session, January 21, 2010,* (Washington, D.C.: U.S. G.P.O., 2010), v.

9 Ibid, 6.

10 Dylan Stableford, "Ray Kelly not surprised about Boston Marathon terror attack," *Yahoo! News | The Lookout*, May 7, 2013, http://news.yahoo.com/blogs/lookout/nypd-ray-kelly-boston-marathon-bombings-173922894.html.

11 Ibid.

12 Daniel Goure, "Countering the Asymmetric Threat from Sea Mines," (Arlington, VA: Lexington Institute), 2010, 10.

13 Albert M. Bottoms and Clyde L. Scandrett, "Applications of Technology to Demining: An Anthology of Scientific Papers (1995-2005)," (Alexandria: *Society for Counter-Ordnance Technology)*, 2005, i.

14 Milan N. Vego, "Operational Warfare at Sea: Theory and Practice," (London: Routledge, 2009), 21-35.

15 Program Executive Office for Littoral and Mine Warfare, *21st Century U.S. Navy Mine Warfare Ensuring Global Access and Commerce,* (Washington, D.C.: Department of the Navy, 2009), 7.

16 Truver. "Mines and Underwater IEDs in U.S. Ports and Waterways: Context, Threats, Challenges, and Solutions," 109.

17 Marvin Heinze, "Maritime Homeland Defense / Security Mine Countermeasures," *Mine Warfare Association*, Last modified May 11, 2011, http://www.minwara.org /Meetings/2011_05/Presentations/wedpdf/0930/CAPT_Heinze_0930.pdf

18 Chief of Naval Operations, *U.S. Navy in "Desert Shield" / "Desert Storm"* (Ser OO/lU500179, 15 May 1991), Chapter V.

19 Tamara Moser Melia, "Lesson That Never Stays Learned," *Mine Warfare Association.* http://www.minwara.org/history-locker/lesson_that_never_stays_learned/, (accessed on May 8, 2013).

[20] David Gerace, "AMCM IPT DEC2012," PowerPoint presentation, AMCM Integrated Product Team Meeting, Norfolk, VA, December 4, 2012.

[21] Ibid.

[22] Scott C. Truver, "Taking Mines Seriously: Mine Warfare in China's Near Seas," *Naval War College Review* Vol. 65 no. 2 (Spring 2012), 61.

[23] United States Navy Fact File, *Mine Countermeasures Ships*, last modified November 7, 2012. http://www.navy.mil/navydata/fact_display.asp?cid=4200&tid=1900&ct=4

[24] Bryan Blair, "Two MCMs Redeploy From 5th Fleet AOR, " *U.S. 7th Fleet Public Affairs*, 26 February 2013, http://www.warrior.navy.mil/.

[25] Chief of Naval Operations, *NATOPS Flight Manual Navy Model MH-53E Helicopters; A1-H53ME-NFM-000*, (Patuxent River, MD: Dept. of Navy, 2006), 14-2.

[26] Commanding Officer, Helicopter Mine Countermeasures FOURTEEN, *HELMINERON FOURTEEN INSTRUCTION 3120.2V: Squadron Standard Operations Procedures*, (Norfolk, VA: HELMINERON FOURTEEN, 2013), 16.

[27] Sam Lagrone, "The US Navy's Combat Ineffective Mine Warfare Force," *Information Dissemination*, October 4, 2011, http://www.informationdissemination.net /2011/10/us-navys-combat-ineffective-mine.html.

[28] The White House. *National Security Strategy*, 18.

[29] Chief of Naval Operations, *Naval Doctrine Publication. 1 Naval Warfare*, (Washington, D.C.: U.S. Dept. of the Navy, 2010), 51-55.

[30] Stephen Roundtree and Sam Forman, "Strait of Hormuz: The World's Key Oil Choke Point," National Geographic, http://environment.nationalgeographic.com/environment /energy/great-energy-challenge/strait-of-hormuz/, (accessed on May 3, 2013).

[31] Ibid.

[32] Scott Truver, "Iranian Mines in the Strait of Hormuz not 'Showstoppers.'" *USNI News*, July 17, 2012. http://news.usni.org/2012/07/17/iranian-mines-strait-hormuz-not-showstoppers#more-373.

[33] Ibid.

[34] Roundtree and Forman, "Strait of Hormuz".

[35] Truver, "Mines and Underwater IEDS," 108.

[36] Truver, "Taking Mines Seriously: Mine Warfare in China's Near Seas," 61.

[37] Gerace, "AMCM IPT DEC2012."

[38] Leon E. Panetta and Barack Obama, *Sustaining U.S. Global Leadership: Priorities for 21st Century Defense*, (Washington, D.C.: Dept. of Defense, 2012), 3.

[39] Ibid.

[40] NATO Maritime Command Home Page, http://www.mc.nato.int/org/smg/Pages /default.aspx, (accessed on April 20, 2013).

[41] Chairman, Joint Chiefs of Staff, *Joint Operation Planning*, Joint Publication (JP) 5-0, (Washington, D.C.: Department of Defense, CJCS, August 11, 2011), 37.

[42] The White House. *National Security Strategy*, 1.

[43] Chief of Naval Operations, *U.S. Navy in "Desert Shield" / "Desert Storm"* (Ser OO/lU500179, May 15, 1991), Chapter VI.

[44] Ibid.

45 Paul Fiddian, "Osprey Minehunters for ROC Navy," *Armed Forces International News,* June 8, 2012, http://www.armedforces-int.com/news/osprey-minehunters-for-roc-navy.html.

Bibliography

Blair, Bryan. "Two MCMs Redeploy From 5th Fleet AOR." *U.S. 7th Fleet Public Affairs,*
February 26, 2013. http://www.warrior.navy.mil/.

Bottoms, Albert M., and Clyde L. Scandrett "Applications of Technology to Demining:
An Anthology of Scientific Papers (1995-2005)." Alexandria: *Society for
Counter-Ordnance Technology*, 2005.

Chief of Naval Operations. *A Cooperative Strategy for 21st Century Seapower.*
Washington, DC: United States Department of the Navy, 2007.

---. *NATOPS Flight Manual, Navy Model MH-53E Helicopters; A1-H53ME-NFM-000.*
Patuxent River, MD: Dept. of Navy, 2006.

---. *Naval Doctrine Publication. 1 Naval Warfare*. Washington, D.C.: U.S. Dept. of the
Navy, 2010.

---. *U.S. Navy in "Desert Shield" / "Desert Storm."* Ser OO/lU500179, 1991.

Chairman, Joint Chiefs of Staff. *Joint Operation Planning.* Joint Publication (JP) 5-0.
Washington, D.C.: Department of Defense, CJCS, August 11, 2011.

---. *Homeland Defense.* Joint Publication (JP) 3-27. Washington, DC: Department of
Defense, CJCS, July 12, 2007.

Commanding Officer, Helicopter Mine Countermeasures FOURTEEN. *HELMINERON
FOURTEEN INSTRUCTION 3120.2V: Squadron Standard Operations
Procedures.* Norfolk, VA: April 1, 2013.

Committee on Foreign Relations, United States Senate. *Al Qaeda in Yemen and Somalia
a Ticking Time Bomb: A Report to the Committee on Foreign Relations, United
States Senate, One Hundred Eleventh Congress, Second Session, January 21,
2010.* Washington, D.C.: U.S. G.P.O., 2010.

Fiddian, Paul. "Osprey Minehunters for ROC Navy." *Armed Forces International News,*
June 8, 2012. http://www.armedforces-int.com/news/osprey-minehunters-for-roc-
navy.html.

Gerace, David. "AMCM IPT DEC2012." PowerPoint presentation. AMCM Integrated
Product Team Meeting, Norfolk, VA. December 4, 2012.

Goure, Daniel. "Countering the Asymmetric Threat from Sea Mines." Arlington, VA:
Lexington Institute, 2010.

Heinze, Marvin. "Maritime Homeland Defense / Security Mine Countermeasures." *Mine Warfare Association.* Last modified 11 May 2011. http://www.minwara.org /Meetings /2011_05/Presentations/wedpdf/0930/CAPT_Heinze_0930.pdf

Lagrone, Sam. "The US Navy's Combat Ineffective Mine Warfare Force." *Information Dissemination*, October 4, 2011. http://www.informationdissemination.net /2011/10/us-navys-combat-ineffective-mine.html.

Melia, Tamara Moser. "Lesson That Never Stays Learned." *Mine Warfare Association.* http://www.minwara.org/history-locker/lesson_that_never_stays_learned/. (accessed on May 8, 2013).

National Geospatial Intelligence Agency. *Distances Between Ports.* Bethesda, MD: National Geospatial Intelligence Agency, 2001. http://l36.com/navigation /Pub151bk.pdf.

NATO Maritime Command Home Page. http://www.mc.nato.int/org/smg/Pages /default.aspx. (accessed on April 20, 2013).

Panetta, Leon E., and Barack Obama. *Sustaining U.S. Global Leadership: Priorities for 21st Century Defense.* Washington, D.C.: Dept. of Defense, 2012.

Program Executive Office for Littoral and Mine Warfare. *21st Century U.S. Navy Mine Warfare Ensuring Global Access and Commerce.* Washington, D.C.: Department of the Navy, 2009.

Roundtree, Stephen and Sam Forman. "Strait of Hormuz: The World's Key Oil Choke Point." *National Geographic.* http://environment.nationalgeographic.com /environment/energy/great-energy-challenge/strait-of-hormuz/. (accessed on May 3, 2013).

Stableford, Dylan. "Ray Kelly not surprised about Boston Marathon terror attack." *Yahoo! News | The Lookout*, May 7, 2013. http://news.yahoo.com/blogs/lookout /nypd-ray-kelly-boston-marathon-bombings-173922894.html.

Tempest, Mark. "Port Security: Sea Mines, UWIEDS and Other Threats." *EagleSpeak.* May 1, 2008. http://observer.guardian.co.uk/waronterrorism/story /0,1373,624278,00.html

The White House. *National Security Strategy.* Washington, D.C.: GPO, 2010.

Truver, Scott C. "Iranian Mines in the Strait of Hormuz not 'Showstoppers'." *USNI News*, July 17, 2012. http://news.usni.org/2012/07/17/iranian-mines-strait-hormuz-not-showstoppers#more-373.

---. "Mines and Underwater IEDs in U.S. Ports and Waterways: Context, Threats, Challenges, and Solutions." *Naval War College Review* Vol. 61 no.1 (Winter 2008). 106-127.

---. "Taking Mines Seriously: Mine Warfare in China's Near Seas." *Naval War College Review* Vol. 65 no. 2 (Spring 2012). 30-66.

United States Navy Fact File. *Mine Countermeasures Ships*. Last modified November 7, 2012. http://www.navy.mil/navydata/fact_display.asp?cid=4200&tid=1900&ct=4.

Vego, Milan N. "Operational Warfare at Sea: Theory and Practice." London: Routledge, 2009.